No Longer Trapped

Pushing Forward

Stephanie Halbert

Copyright © 2018 Stephanie Halbert

All rights reserved. No part of this publication may be reproduced, distributed, or transmitted in any form or by any means, including photocopying, recording, or other electronic or mechanical methods, without the prior written permission of the publisher, except in the case of brief quotations embodied in critical reviews and certain other noncommercial uses permitted by copyright law.

All Scriptures are taken from the Authorized King James Bible. The KJV is public domain in the United States.

ISBN: 978-1-7326934-2-5

Liberation's Publishing LLC
West Point, Mississippi

Dedication

This book is dedicated to

my lovely kids, Mya, Elijah, and Elisha Halbert, who push and encourage me not to settle for less

my dear mother, Dorothy Halbert, who taught and raised me to be the woman I am today

Stephanie Halbert

Contents

Personal Encounter 11

A Praise in My Heart 17

Stay Focused 21

Expect More 25

No Longer Bound 29

Faith Moves God 33

Know Your Worth 37

Forgive and Move Forward 41

You Are God's Favorite 45

Look Beyond the Ordinary 49

Soldier, Rise Up 55

Stephanie Halbert

My mom is a very encouraging woman of God. She has inspired so many people, and she has lead them in the right direction while on her journey as she walked by faith with God.

~Mya Halbert

She's pure in heart. The day this book is released the nation will change! God has anointed and blessed a great Evangelist to minister to millions of broken spirits. The weakest points in our lives can change to the strongest. I am presenting to you my friend, my confidant, Stephanie Halbert. This book can change your life.

~Connie Whitefield

She's a Godly woman with a Godly gift. She's been ordained to build up God's kingdom. When I met her, I instantly felt a spirit of excellence, and I saw a warrior. She stands ready to go into battle for others. I see a royal queen with a warm beautiful smile. The love she has for others reaches over the highest mountains. I am glad to be connected to someone with such a high anointing on their life. God has a Master plan and a Master key to lead to the fulfillment thereof .

~Daril Bishop

Stephanie Halbert

Acknowledgement

This book is inspired by the grace of my Lord and Savior Jesus Christ, the love of God and the fellowship of His Holy Spirit. ~2 Corinthians 13:14

Many times we go through life with a silent cry for help. We carry that fake smile. We act like everything is going well, and it seems like we have it all together. In reality, we are dying inside from the weight of the world. Bills are due, children are acting out, job and school are stressful. There's sickness on every hand, depression and suicidal thoughts, money is low and families are falling apart.

Sometimes the weight of the world can be too much to bear. We get so caught up in our adversities that we fail to realize who God is and what He is truly able to do. We become victims of our minds. Our mind has us trapped in our situations, in our conditions and in our circumstances. This book is to inspire you to keep pushing forward, regardless of what you are faced with. Be set free and no longer be your own worst enemy.

Personal Encounter

I can truly say that my life has been great. Of course I had some cloudy days, but my good days outweigh the bad days. Whatever I was faced with, I was able to overcome it by the grace of my Lord and Savior Jesus Christ.

However, life can sometimes bring you situations that can shake your confidence. It can make you doubt yourself and doubt God. I got to a time in my life where I was faced with many adversities and many "can't do's" to the point where I felt like giving up.

This may sound crazy, but I felt so close to God, that I knew, without a shadow of a doubt, if I would have spoken the words "Lord, I'm tired", I knew, He would have taken me home to glory with Him.

I was tired; I felt weighed down, beaten and broken. The weight of the world seemed so hard for me to bear. I felt like giving up, but I had three precious, beautiful, children who looked up to me and who were depending on me.

One day I was sitting at my kitchen table crying, tears just falling. I couldn't see my way out of my situations and yes I said situations. I never felt this low in my 40 years of life.

It felt like it was easier to give up, instead of giving my problems to God. I said I trust Him, but my actions showed something different. I knew one fact, I knew I needed God. I had done everything I knew to do.

Sitting there in tears the Spirit of God spoke to me saying " If you spend the same energy and faith you have in giving up and use that same energy and faith in trusting and believing in me, you will see a shift in your situations. I can make your burdens light. I came through for you before. I will do it again. There is nothing too hard for Me. I am God. The Beginning and the End. The Truth and the Life."

I pondered on that night and day. As I was asleep one night, I was awakened to what seemed to be a dream, but it seemed so real. I was laying there in bed worshipping and praising God. I felt a presence with me, but that didn't stop my praise and worship. After a while the praising and worshipping stopped, and there was quietness and darkness. Shortly after, I was in front of this very bright light, and a voice spoke to me saying "Go back". I suddenly woke up. I came out of that dream still feeling the emotions. I felt so close to God during that experience. It felt like I was right there in God's presence.

This showed me that God controls everything including life and death. There's nothing that can happen unless God allows it. I changed my mindset. Even though I was faced with many hurdles to cross; I knew who was in control. There were so many other situations where God showed me He was with me. I remember a time when I had this bill due, but I didn't have the money to pay it. I thought, ok I'll borrow it from my sister and repay her back. Then I thought, well I don't want to do that. I don't want my family all in my business, but

God had a plan far from what my eyes could see or ears could hear. My sister called me and asked me about the bill that I had to pay. She told me to come by her job. She was going to write me a check, and I didn't have to pay her back.

PRAISE BREAK

God said you thought of a plan, but I had something better. I'll have her to contact you about YOUR bill, give you the money to pay it, and you will not have to pay her back. Look at God... Won't He do it! As it states in Philippians 4:19 "But my God shall supply all your needs according to His riches in glory by Christ Jesus." (KJV)

At that moment I prayed and surrendered all my being to God. It was no more excuses for me. I knew the power of God. I knew what He was able and capable of doing. Prayer changes things. God can do anything but fail. He can fix any situation, any circumstance, or condition. He can turn your no's into yes's and your sorrow into praise.

As the song writer says, Trouble don't last always. Weeping may endure for the nigh,t but JOY comes in the morning. HOLD ON TO GOD'S UNCHANGING HAND BECAUSE the storm that was used to break you, will be the storm God uses to make you. THE DEVIL THOUGHT HE WAS WINNING BUT GOD FLIPPED THE SCRIPT.

A Praise in My Heart

As Psalm 86:12 states, "I will praise thee, O Lord my God, with all my heart and I will glorify thy name for evermore."(KJV) I owe God all the praise, because if it had not been for the Lord on my side where would I be. I have to keep a praise in my heart. A lot of times I had to praise my way through my situations. As I was going through the difficult times in my life, songs like *God's Favor* by Donald Lawrence blessed my soul.

I thank God for His favor and for keeping me. One of my favorite parts of the song speaks about never doubting. God can turn things around. All things are possible with God. God is wonderful. God is marvelous, and He is an on time God.

There was this one situation I was going through where the song Way Maker kept singing in my spirit. When I thought of my situation, I started singing the lyrics of, *Way Maker by* Sinach. She sings about God being a miracle worker, and a light in darkness. While singing that song, I was encouraging myself, reminding myself who God is. It helped me to get through my situation. I was spiritually strengthened while I glorified God.

I'm reminded of the lyrics of *I'm Getting Ready* by Tasha Cobb. The song is based off of a familiar scripture 1 Corinthians 2:19 "But as it is written, Eye hath not seen, nor ear heard, neither have entered into the heart of man, the things which God hath prepared for them that love him." (KJV) I truly believe that God allows us to get to a low season in our life, so He can bring us back better than before.

She sings about Overflow! God will open up windows of heaven and pour out blessings that there shall not be room enough to receive. God loves all of us. He doesn't want to see us down and out. If we can only see ourselves through the eyes of our Lord and Savior Jesus Christ. We are individuals that are strong and courageous. As Deuteronomy 31:6 states "Be strong and of a good courage, fear not, nor be afraid of them: for the LORD thy God, he *it is* that doth go with thee; he will not fail thee, nor forsake thee." (KJV)

Stephanie Halbert

Stay Focused

We allow ourselves to get so distracted by the things of the world. In Romans 12:2 it states, "And be not conformed to this world: but be ye transformed by the renewing of your mind, that ye may prove what is that good, and acceptable, and perfect, will of God." (KJV)

I remember when I decided to take a break from Facebook®. I noticed that I was on Facebook® more than I was reading the word of God or talking to Him. So I decided to take a break from it. It had become so common for me to browse my timeline, that I found myself just automatically logging onto Facebook® without realizing it. I thought to myself, if I pick up my bible and read it or just trust in the Lord with all my heart as much as I logged into social media what would my life really be like. My normal or the things that are common definitely had to change.

So many things in this world can be a distraction. Our mindset and way of thinking has to change. God tells us if we keep our mind stayed on Him, he will keep us in perfect peace. His word is true. He is a God that will not lie.

I'm reminded of Psalm 56:8 when David said, "Thou tellest my wanderings: put thou my tears into thy bottle: are they not in thy book?"(KJV). David was going through a difficult time like we all sometimes go through. Like David we want God to remember us.

At that point in the bible the Philistines had captured David. When David wrote this Psalm he was a prisoner of war. In our life we feel like we are out on the battlefield. We are faced with so many adversities. It sometimes feels like a whole army is attacking us. In this Psalm David stayed focused inspite of everything going on around him. He was so confident that God was for him. He encouraged himself, in God he trusted and he was not afraid.

That is the way we should be as believers regardless of what we are facing. Stay focused and encourage yourself, and know that God is with you. There is NO weapon formed that will prosper. I heard this quotes by an unknown author, *What consumes your mind controls your life;* That being said don't focus on your adversaries. Focus on God's possibilities.

Stephanie Halbert

Expect More

We have to change our expectations. We must change the way we think and view situations. Don't just expect the ordinary or the natural blessings. Expect the supernatural and expect the unordinary. God wants to do something so amazing in our lives. He wants to bless us far beyond what our natural eyes can see. He wants to give us that explosive blessing.

I heard of a person who grew up in a family with just enough to make ends meet. As he got older he was determined to make something out of himself. He didn't want his future to be like his past, like it was for him growing up. He wanted more. He looked beyond what his natural eyes had seen. He looked beyond the ordinary. His eyes were on the supernatural and the unordinary.

He was born and raised in church, and he knew the power God. He knew if he would just keep his hands in God's hand, there was nothing that God could not and would not do. All through his childhood and adulthood, he kept his faith and believed in God. He grew up to be a successful man. Married with kids.

It seemed like whatever he desired for himself or his family they were blessed with it. He has a nice big home, several cars, and a good amount of savings in his bank account. I am sure there were some rocky days. Some days he may have felt like giving up, but he did not. The bottom line is that

God's desire is to bless us and to bless us abundantly. Our faith moves God not our situations.

Stephanie Halbert

No Longer Bound

I know you've heard the saying from Arthur Fletcher "A mind is a terrible thing to waste." The truth of the matter is "it is". Don't waste your mind with thoughts of doubts, defeats, or negative thinking. Nurture your mind with thoughts of successes, with I cans and I wills. You have to train your mind to think about positive and good things and not about bad things. In Proverbs 23:7 it says "For as he thinketh in his heart, so is he: Eat and drink, saith he to thee; but his heart is not with thee."(KJV)

When there's a problem the first thing you have to do is to acknowledge it. You acknowledge the fact that it's your own thoughts that are holding you back from your destiny. Acknowledge the fact that you are chickened out because in your mind you are afraid of the naysayers, the can't doers, the that will never happeners. The ones who think you're crazy to think things will come to past.

Yes, it's you! The thoughts in your mind. Now say enough is enough. I will no longer be trapped in my own mind. I will no longer let the words of others control my way of thinking, the storm is over. I'm pushing forward. I'm no longer trapped. Believe in yourself, because when God is for you who can be against you?

In 3 John 1:2 says "Beloved, I wish above all things that thou mayest prosper and be in health, even as thy soul prospereth." (KJV) Our Heavenly Father wishes prosperity and good health over our lives. Why is it so hard for us to speak life into ourselves? He tells us in John 14:12 Verily, verily, I say unto you, He that believeth on me, the works that I do shall he do also; and greater works than these shall he do; because I go unto my Father."(KJV)

Take the limits off of God. Use the power that lies within. Let me give you this analogy, if you visually look at a match, visually it's a wooden stick with a red tip. Within it's more than that. The Wikipedia dictionary describes a match as "a small wooden stick or stiff paper. One end is coated with a material that can be ignited by frictional heat generated by striking the match against a suitable surface." https://en.wikipedia.org/wiki/Match

The match looks small to the natural eye with no value, but once you learn its ability you then know it's of much value. When it's struck against a suitable surface it ignites.

Watch this, people might look on you as someone of no value. They may even have said you would never accomplish anything. You're a waste of life. However, when your life mixes with the Holy Spirit and the Holy Spirit abides in you,

My God, My God....

Let me encourage you, in Romans 8:37 states, "Yet in all these things we are more than conquerors through Him who loved us."(KJV) You can conquer everything you put your mind to. Have faith and believe that it can be done, and it will. In Matthew 19:26 is says, "But Jesus beheld them, and said unto them, With men this is impossible; but with God all things are possible."(KJV)

Faith Moves God

Training your mind is just an act of faith. In Hebrews 11:1 it states, "**NOW** faith is the substance of things hoped for and the evidence of things not seen." (KJV) Simply put, faith is trusting in something you cannot openly prove or see. Trust is relying on the fact that something is true.

We often heard of the illustration of the chair. A chair is designed to support a person who sits on it. Trust is actually sitting in the chair because you believe it will not collapse. Understanding and acting in faith is crucial. In Hebrews 11: 6 it tells us without faith it is impossible to please God. **God moves by our faith.** Let's take the woman with the issue of blood, in Luke 8:43 the woman had an issue of blood for twelve long years. She had spent all her living upon physicians, neither could heal her. She heard that Jesus was coming to town. I believed she had pre-destined faith. She knew if she could just touch Him, any part of Him she would be made whole. "**O my God, what strong faith this is!**"

This woman came and just touched the HEM of Jesus' garment. In Luke 8:44 it states she came behind and touched the border of his garment and **IMMEDIATELY** her issue of bleeding stopped. Her faith was so strong that Jesus felt the faith she had through His garment.

In Luke 8:45-46 states "And Jesus said, Who touched me? When all denied, Peter and they that were with him said, Master, the multitude throng thee and press thee, and sayest thou, Who touched me? 46 And Jesus said, Somebody hath touched me: for I perceive that virtue is gone out of me." (KJV)

The woman came to Jesus, falling down before him, declaring unto him that she had touched him and how she was healed immediately. Jesus said to her your **faith** hath made you whole.

This story shows that God is moved by our faith. If we have faith the size of a mustard seed, we can speak to mountains and tell mountains be ye removed. With faith, nothing is impossible. With faith we can walk in the abundance of the Lord. With faith we can face the giants that are within us that plague our minds.

Faith gives us strength, meaning the inner strength to fight off the battle within our mind. Faith gives you courage. Faith in God provides stability. As Proverbs 3:5-6 states, "Trust in the LORD with all thine heart; and lean not unto thine own understanding. 6 In all thy ways acknowledge him, and he shall direct thy paths." (KJV) Walk in your destiny. There is nothing too hard for God. Just trust Him. He is able.

Know Your Worth

I know you might often find a penny lying around on the ground. Some may pick it up, while some may just leave it there. Some leave it there, because in their mind they might think "O it's only a penny. It's only worth one cent." It can be worth a lot if you look at it differently. If you only have 49 pennies you need one more to make fifty cents. If you have 99 pennies you need one more to make a dollar.

Don't lose your blessings looking at things from the natural eye. For in 1 Corinthians 2:9 "But as it is written, Eye hath not seen, nor ear heard, neither have entered into the heart of man, the things which God hath prepared for them that love him." (KJV) Your way and your purpose is already prepared. God has a plan for you. In Jeremiah 29:11 says "For I know the thoughts that I think toward you, saith the LORD, thoughts of peace, and not of evil, to give you an expected end." (KJV)

Know your worth. Your self-worth is what you think about yourself; it's not the opinion of what others think about you. You are not what the devil says you are. When the devil says you're one thing you say you are not that.

In Matthew 10:31 it tells us, "Fear ye not therefore, ye are of more value than many sparrows." (KJV) God loves you above all things. He tells us in John 3:16 "For God so loved the world that he gave his only begotten son, that whosoever believeth in Him should not perish but have everlasting life." (KJV)

In Romans 5:8 states "But God commendeth his love toward us, in that, while we were yet sinners, Christ died for us." (KJV) You mean more to God, more than you could ever think. So don't waste your time in doubting about anything. If you keep your mind stayed on God, He will keep you in perfect peace. God thought you were worth dying for.

Set your goals for your life. Even though you might have people in your life who don't believe in you or your vision, you believe in your own vision. Change your way of thinking. When God is for you who can be against you? There is no limit. He tells us that we have not because we ask not. In Philippians 4:6 He tells us "Be careful for nothing; but in everything by prayer and supplication with thanksgiving let your requests be made known unto God." (KJV)

Forgive and Move Forward

In order to completely move forward and no longer be trapped, you have to forgive those who hurt you. You have to forgive yourself. Forgiveness is not always easy. Most times before we forgive we want to get even. We want to do unto others as they did unto us. But forgiveness is one of the best healing procedures a person can do. As Ephesians 4:31-32 states "31 Let all bitterness, and wrath, and anger, and clamour, and evil speaking, be put away from you, with all malice: 32 And be ye kind one to another, tenderhearted, forgiving one another, even as God for Christ's sake hath forgiven you." (KJV)

None of us are perfect, but we do serve a perfect God. Let the past hurts and disappointments go. Forgive and move forward. Be no longer trapped. Set yourself free. Hanging on to bitterness is only another sign of someone else controlling you. When you are hanging on to your past hurts, disappointments, failures, past sins or let downs you are only allowing the works of the past to control your future destiny.

Take control of your thinking and forgive, and be set free. Turn your pain to fame. Turn your bitterness to sweetness, and choose forgiveness over bitterness and be set free. In John 8:36 it states, "If the Son therefore shall make you free, ye shall be free indeed." (KJV)

God is a forgiving God. He's not concerned about your yesterdays or yesteryears. So why do you continue to think in the past? Repentance is our chain breaker from our past. So don't allow your mind or others to hold you in bondage of your past. 1 John 1:9 says "If we confess our sins, he is faithful and just to forgive us our sins, and to cleanse us from all unrighteousness." (KJV)

Now if God can forgive us, why not forgive ourselves? Stop holding on to it. Whatever your "IT" is let "IT" go. No matter what we have done the forgiveness is there. God is our Father, and He is a forgiving Father. There is nothing too big that God cannot fix. All we have to do is believe and trust Him. Whatever you are guilty of God can forgive. Once God forgives, then forgive yourself. Do not pick that garbage back up.

Think about it, once you set your garbage out for the sanitation workers to pick up, you don't go to the landfill to reclaim it do you? No, of course you don't. I haven't seen anyone do that in my 40 years of life. So, the garbage, the toxins that are in your life, once you lay it at the foot of Jesus leave it there. Don't reclaim it. Learn that the battle is not yours; it's the Lord. In John 14:1 He tells us to let not our heart be troubled. He wants us to be at peace.

Get up, dust yourself off and move forward. Since you are no longer trapped, you are no longer connected to your past sins, your past hurts or your past disappointments; you are no longer connected to anything that's holding you in bondage. Let nothing keep you from the many blessings God has for you. **You are no longer trapped. You are pushing forward.**

You Are God's Favorite

God favors you. You are one of His precious jewels. God sent His son to die for you, because He thought you were worth it. So take the shackles off, and be set free. Take the shackles off in your mind, and be free. For we all have sinned and come short of His glory, but thank God. We have a way out through repentance. The way has already been made. All you have to do is walk in it.

Free your mind. Free yourself so you can live the abundant life God has for you. The debt has already been paid. God sent Jesus to die for our sins, so we wouldn't have to. So why continue to torment yourself. You are God's favorite so, Let it go. Enough is enough; it's time to push forward.

I know this is easier said than done. But the truth of the matter is, it can be done. Control your thinking. In Isaiah 26:3 states "Thou wilt keep him in perfect peace, whose mind is stayed on thee: because he trusteth in thee." (KJV) Having a freed mind is so enjoyable. It's good for you and the people around you. Allow God to take control. He can do so much better with things that bother you than you can.

There was this couple who was going through this nasty divorce. They both sought Christian counseling, but their minds were boggled down by the divorce. They were worried so much about what people would think of them. The couple were more people pleasers than God pleasers. That is until one day reality hit. They were a couple who truly loved each other and who truly loved God. It wasn't until they took their mind off of pleasing people that they were able to restore their marriage.

With them changing their mindset they were able to restore their marriage and rekindle the love that they once had before. All we have to do is trust God and keep the faith. He tells us in Hebrews 13:5 that he will never leave you or forsake you. If God is always with us, and He will never leave, or forsake us, why is it so hard to just completely trust Him? He wants what is best for us. His desires for us are so much more than what our eyes could see or our mind could think. That's in **EVERY** situation we go through. Whether it's relationship, work, home, or school, he wants our mind to be at peace, and he wants us to allow Him to take over.

Can you imagine if you were to just surrender your whole being to God? What would your life really be like. When a situation occurs, instead of worrying, just say, "Lord you fix it;" and really believe and trust that He would do just that, fix it. Do you know how much peace you will have? It's just indescribable. God is good, and He is waiting for us to just turn everything over to Him. He doesn't want us to be trapped, unfocused, or not living our full potential. We are His favorite. He wants us to be free as a dove, living life to the fullest, doing the work in which He has commanded us. Life is beautiful, so why not live a beautiful, stress free life.

Look Beyond the Ordinary

I'm reminded of this little girl who grew up in a single parent home. She always thought she was less than, because she didn't come from a two parent home or a home with morals as some of the world would say. She lived in insecurities. She had low self-esteem; she just didn't have a desire to live her life to the fullest. It was all because she didn't come from a home with a mother and a father. As she got older she went off to college. She learned who God really was; she gave her life to God.

As she studied God's word and learned of Him, she grew in confidence and gained courage. She no longer felt less than. She no longer walked with her head down feeling defeated by the world. She realized that she was blessed with a life of purpose.

It didn't matter what background she came from or who wasn't present in her life. She had a chance to make the best of the life she was given.

All we have to do is use what we have. It doesn't matter who is or who is not present. Once we learn to make the best out of the hand that we are given, our lives become so much better.

There was this husband and wife who had been married for a long time. They had successful children. Their children were all doctors or lawyers. They were a Christian family who truly believed in God. They had a good life, and they were truly blessed.

One day the husband was involved in a terrible accident where he had to be rushed to the hospital for immediate surgery. He had internal bleeding.

The wife prayed and prayed to God to bring her husband out of surgery and that he recovered speedily. The husband died during surgery.

The wife became angry. She was angry with God, and wanted to know why God allowed this to happen. She had been faithful. She prayed and worshiped God daily. She paid her tithes, and she had her kids paying their tithes. She just couldn't wrap her mind around why. She felt like all the things she had done for God should have saved her from this moment. He shouldn't have let this happen to her husband. She spread the good news of God. She fasted, prayed, and tithed. It just didn't seem real that God had allowed this to happen to **<u>HER</u>**.

She felt as if God owed her a favor. One day she met with her Pastor, and she told him how she really felt about God. The Pastor was so stunned at the way she was talking. He couldn't believe the way she was talking in reference to God. She was one of his good members. The Pastor prayed and fasted for her, but it wasn't until she had a reality check.

She realized regardless of what we go through God is still good, and God is still in control. He sits high and He looks low. God allows things to happen for a reason, but he still has his arms wrapped all around us in every situation. God allows things to happen to us to show that He is in control.

Look at Job. Job was a blessed man. He had favor with the Lord. One day God took the hedge from around Job just to prove to Satan that He is still Lord, and that Job would not curse Him and die.

Job lost everything he had, but he did not lose his faith and belief in God. His friends and his spouse thought he should curse God and die, but he did not. He kept the faith.

For that, God blessed Job with twice as much as he had before. God blessed the last part of Job's life more than the first part; and he had fourteen thousand sheep, six thousand camels, a thousand yoke of oxen, and a thousand asses. He also had seven sons and three daughters. And after this Job lived a hundred and forty years.

All we have to do is stay with the Lord. Don't focus on the ordinary, look beyond. We serve a God that never fails. He wants us to be blessed and be blessed more abundantly.

Soldier, Rise Up

There's a soldier inside of you that's waiting to break free, to fulfill the work that God has for you. Even though weeping endures for the night, joy comes in the morning. Your battle has already been **<u>FOUGHT AND WON</u>**. God tells us that the victory is ours. He took our place upon Calvary carrying all the sins we committed along with all the evil we have done. He went unto the Father for us.

Keep moving forward while under attack. God tells us that we have the victory. We are the head and not the tail. So, do not think anything less than that. It does not matter where you've been or what you've been through. You are never too low that

God cannot pick you up. Push toward the mark of the high calling which is Christ Jesus.

What's to come is better than what's been. Keep moving forward while you are under attack, because the battle is not given to the swift nor to the strong, but to the one that endures to the end. Ecclesiastes 9:11 You are a child of the most High King. He has cattle on a thousand hills. You will not lack if you just trust and believe in Him.

He will put the right people in your path. He will make your enemy your footstool. You are not defeated with Christ. This is a battlefield and you are a soldier who has been equipped for battle. Put on the full armor of God. As Ephesians 6:10-18 states be strong in the Lord, and in the power of His might.

God did not bring you this far to leave you. He has been with you always, even until the end of the world. Just trust Him. You are free to live and to receive the complete blessings of God. He is standing with His arm stretched wide waiting on you. There's no better feeling than knowing you are being kept by the blood of Jesus Christ. His blood covers you. So why not become the soldier that lies within you. God has got you covered. If He did it before he can do it again.

God has brought us all through something. Whatever your situation, your condition, or circumstance is or was, I'm sure you can attest with me "IF it had not been for the Lord on my(your) side where would I(you) be.

Continue to have faith, and trust in the Lord. YOU ARE NO LONGER TRAPPED. Continue to push. Push yourself right into your breakthrough. The way has already been made through Christ Jesus. He is the beginning and the end. He is the true and living God. He is able to do exceedingly, and abundantly above all we can ask or think. There's nothing too hard for God. He is a God that CANNOT fail. His mercy is brand new EVERY morning. Just trust Him and sit back and watch Him work.

I'm a living witness that He is Able. Believe That you are no longer trapped. Soldier Rise Up and keep **P**ushing **U**ntil **S**omething **H**appens!

No Longer Trapped   Pushing Forward

Stephanie Halbert

www.ingramcontent.com/pod-product-compliance
Lightning Source LLC
Chambersburg PA
CBHW052118070526
44584CB00017B/2548